GW01191622

To Hold

WORKS BY
Felicity Aylieff
Gordon Baldwin
Alison Britton
Natasha Daintry
Ken Eastman
Morgen Hall
He Jian
Walter Keeler
Bodil Manz
Hylton Nel
Margaret O'Rorke
Martin Smith
Rupert Spira
Julian Stair
Peter Ting
Takeshi Yasuda

CURATED BY
Peter Ting
PHOTOGRAPHS
Jan Baldwin

hold
to hold
to hold
to hold
to hold
to

BRANTWOOD PUBLISHING
London 2006

ISBN 0 9552603 0 2
Published by Brantwood Publishing 2006
Copyright 2006 © Text: Peter Ting and Authors;
Photographs: Jan Baldwin, Additional Photography:
Julian Stair and Peter Ting

Designed by Colin Sackett
Printed and bound by Short Run Press, Exeter

BRANTWOOD PUBLISHING
60 Brantwood Road
London SE24 0DJ

Contents

Introduction   9
Peter Ting

Felicity Aylieff	12	*Bodil Manz*	76
Gordon Baldwin	20	*Hylton Nel*	84
Alison Britton	28	*Margaret O'Rorke*	92
Natasha Daintry	36	*Martin Smith*	100
Ken Eastman	44	*Rupert Spira*	108
Morgen Hall	52	*Julian Stair*	116
He Jian	60	*Peter Ting*	124
Walter Keeler	68	*Takeshi Yasuda*	132

Photographs by Jan Baldwin

Running Commentary   141
Alison Britton and Natasha Daintry

Barrett Marsden   149
Juliana Barrett and Tatjana Marsden

The Collector   155
Harriet K.

To Hold   161
Alun Graves

Contact details and Acknowledgements   167

Introduction *by Peter Ting*

'To hold' is a project where everything came to me all at once,
right at the beginning—the title, the exhibitors, the format of
the book—only missing link was the why. Knowing what was
in my mind would make a visually stimulating and inspirat-
ional exhibition; I eventually realized that 'the why' is my own
passion for ceramics, and specifically the vessel. The exhibitors
range from the well establish to those in mid and early career,
embracing an assortment of techniques.

My collaborator, photographer Jan Baldwin, bravely came
on this voyage with me. Her sensitive eye, firm and gentle
manner caught the best qualities and the 'creative spark'
in each person, which is often seen and felt in face to face
conversations, but so rarely captured on film. This book in the
manner of a photographic journal has allowed us to catch and
to share with you a glimpse into their creative lives.

The commissioned essays trace the journey of a piece of
work, from the germ of an idea, through the studio, the gallery,
and finally to the collector. I hope that you will experience the
same joy and insight I felt, when reading them for the first
time.

'To hold' started as an idea, became a journey and ended
as a pilgrimage. It allowed me the opportunity to visit, talk,
laugh with people whose work I have always respected and
loved. It reaffirms my passion for clay and the vessel, whether
it holds dreams, light, melancholy or a cup of tea.

Felicity Aylieff

BATH, SOMERSET

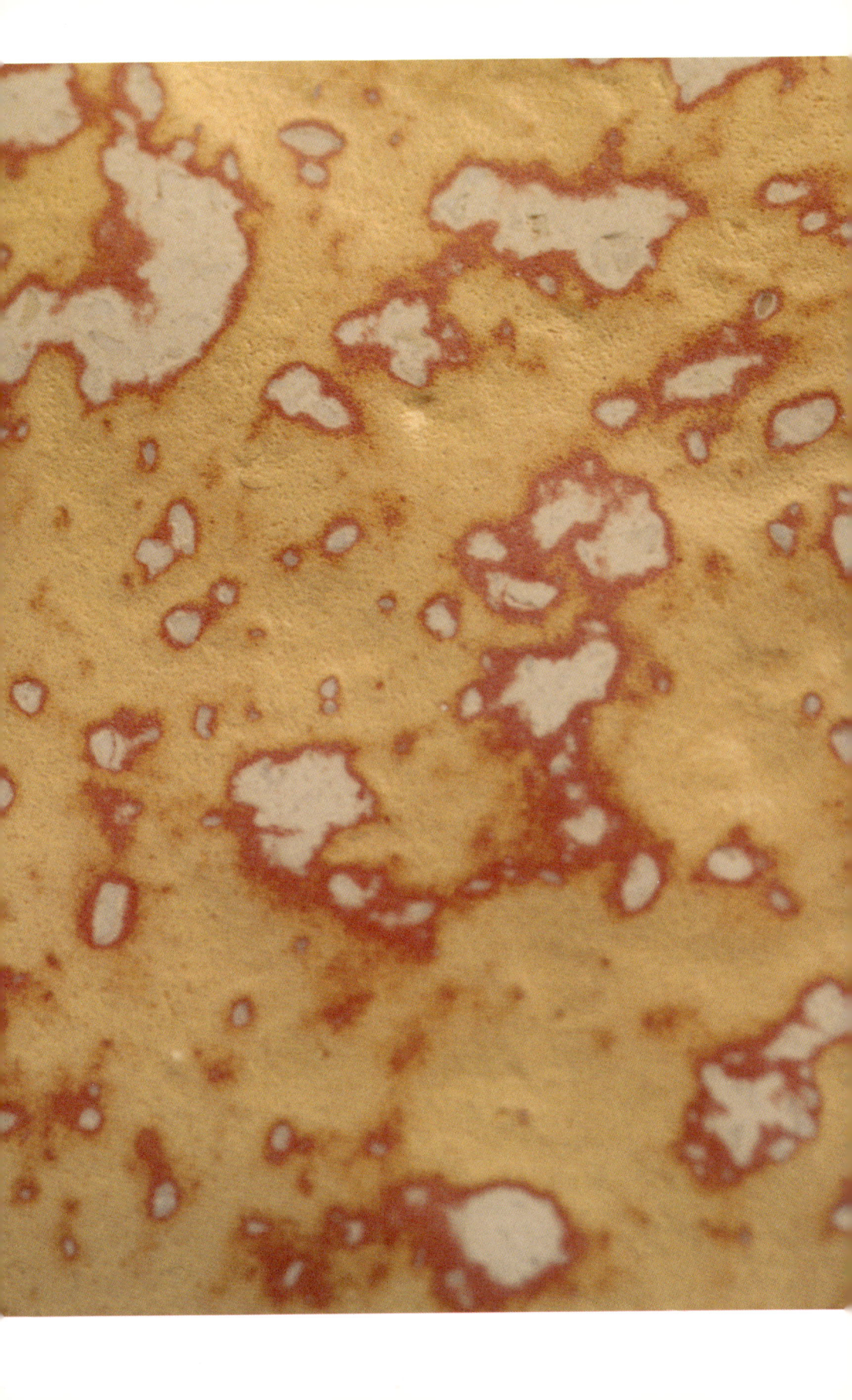

18

Gordon Baldwin

MARKET DRAYTON, SHROPSHIRE

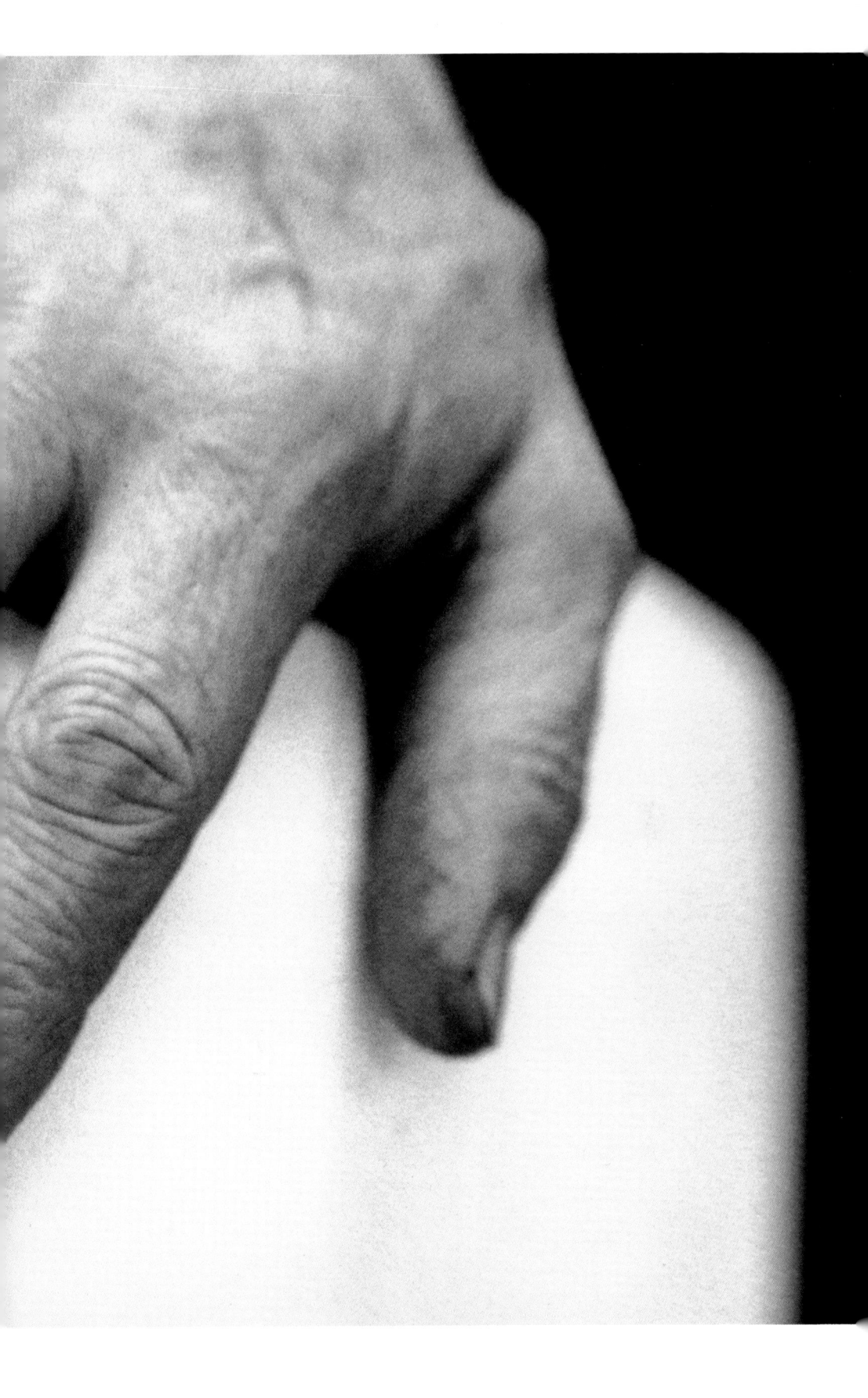

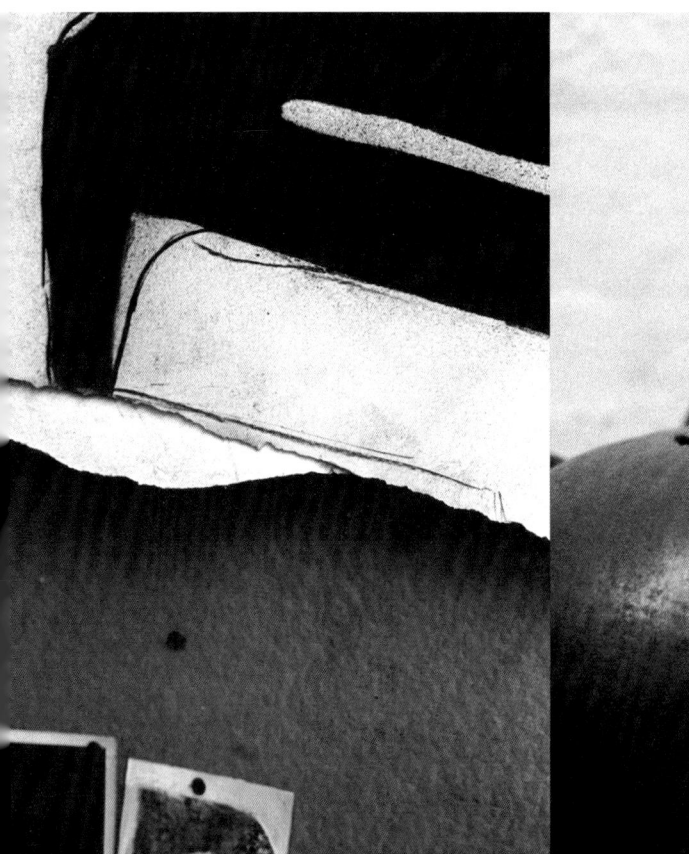

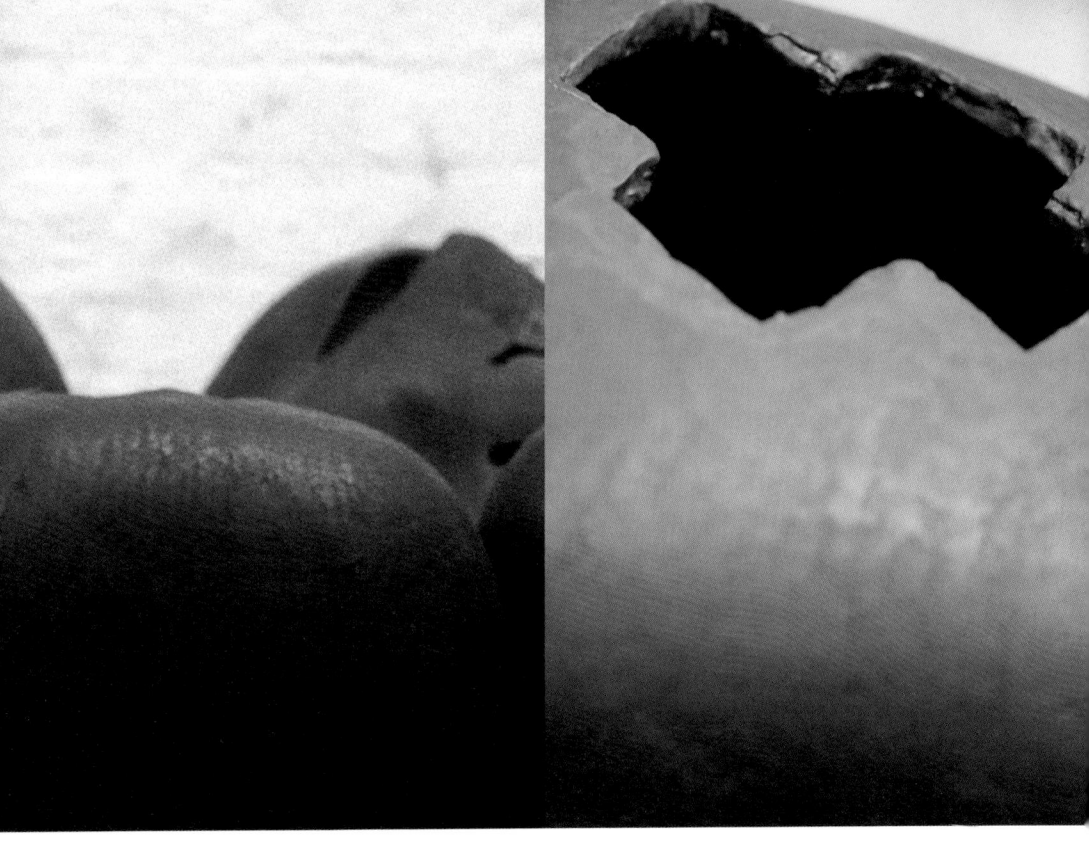

Alison Britton

STOKE NEWINGTON, LONDON

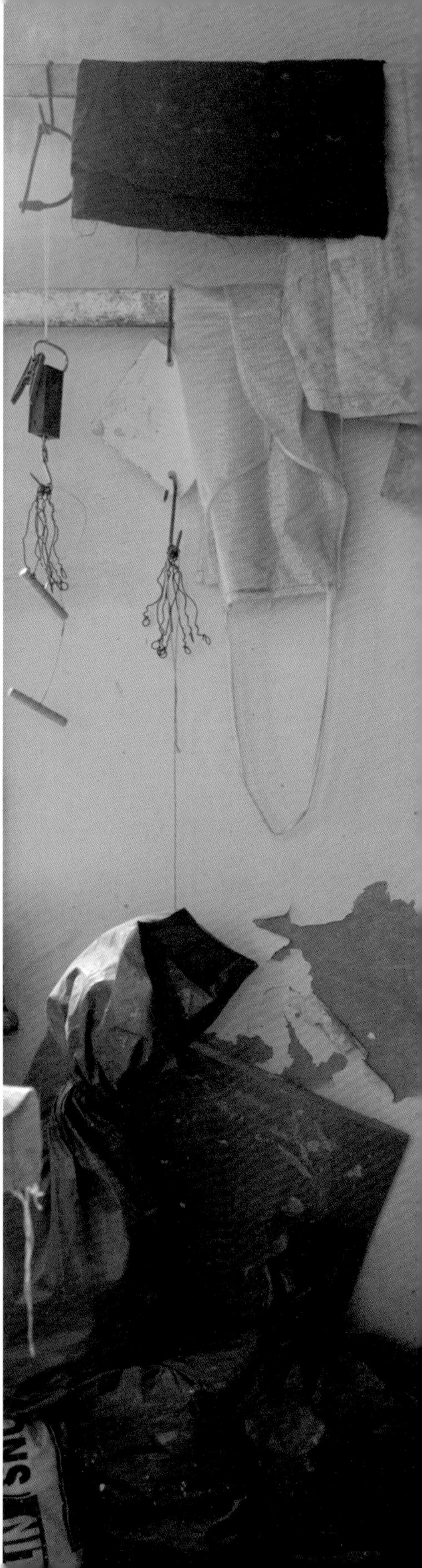

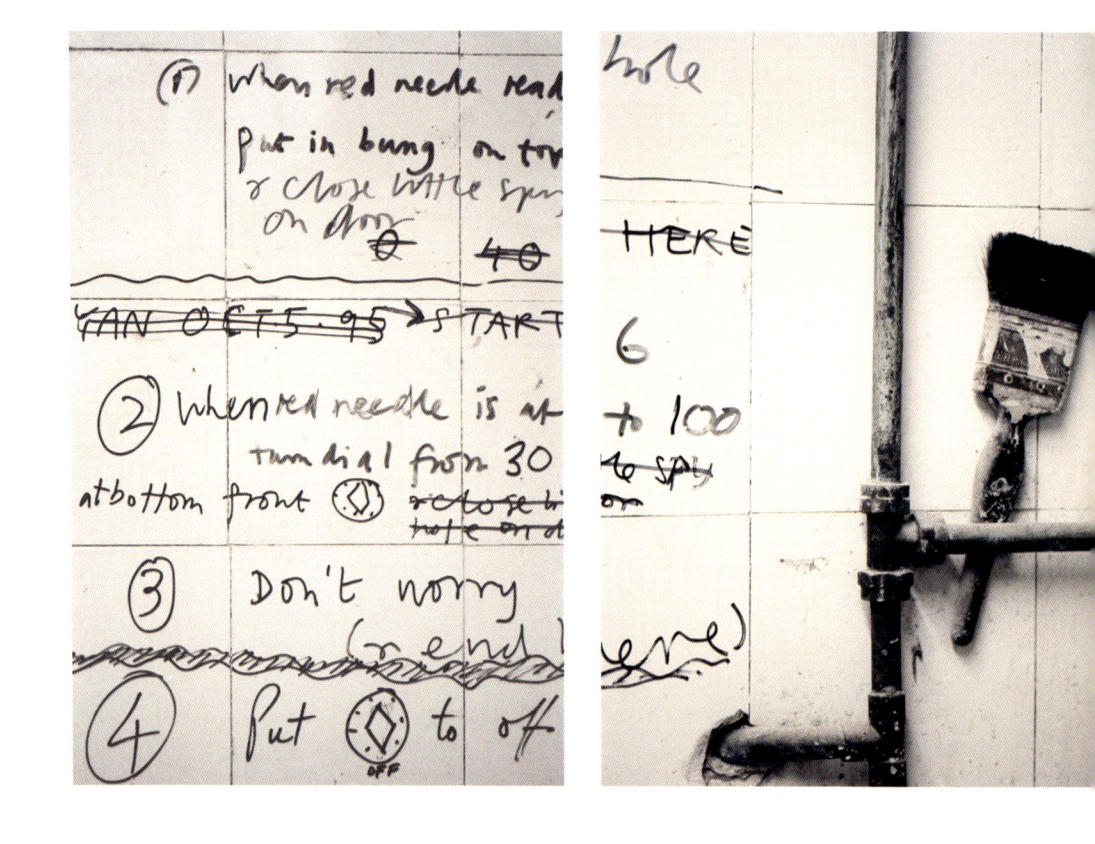

Natasha Daintry

VAUXHALL, LONDON

38

Ken Eastman

Morgen Hall

CARDIFF, WALES

He Jian

SHANGHAI, CHINA

Walter Keeler

PENALLT, MONMOUTHSHIRE

75

Bodil Manz

HØRVE, DENMARK

Hylton Nel

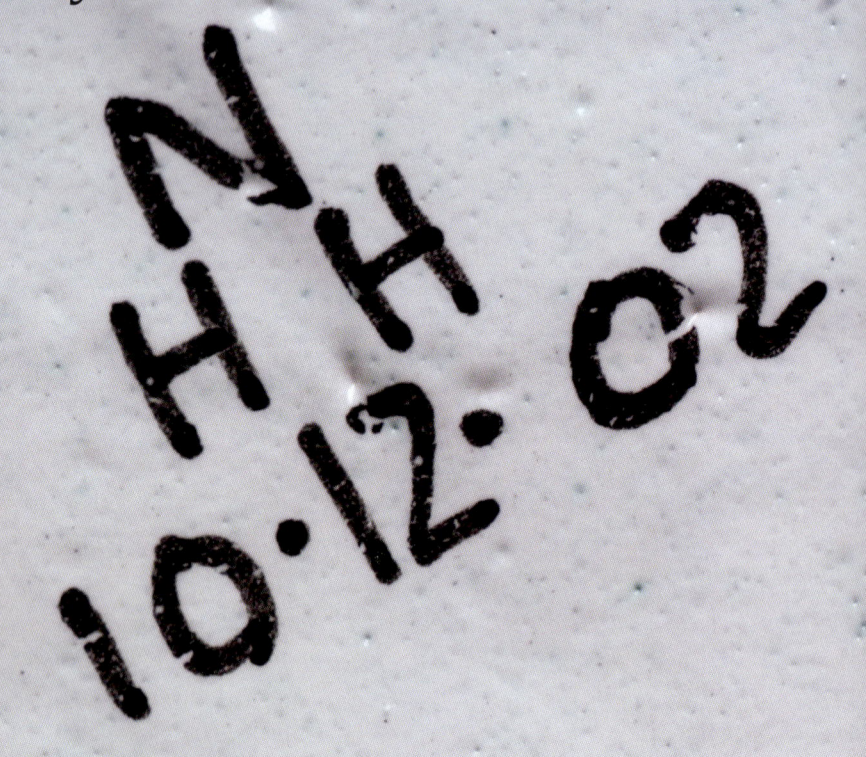

LONDON, UK | CALITZDORP, SOUTH AFRICA

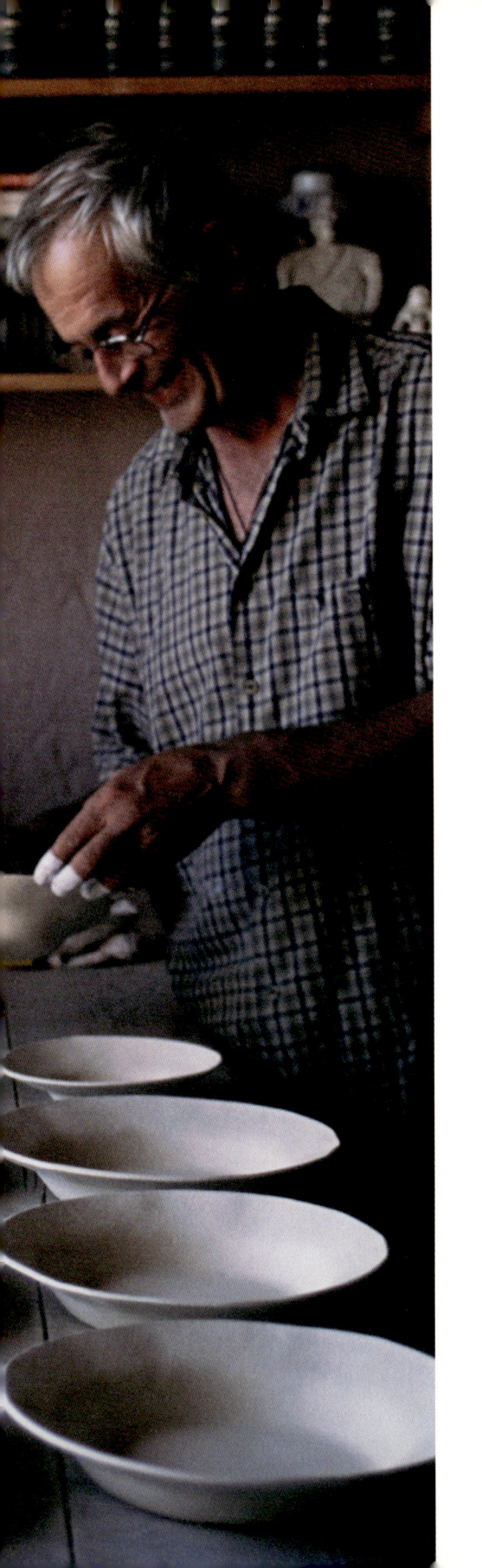

Margaret O'Rorke

OXFORD, OXFORDSHIRE

Martin Smith

CAMDEN TOWN, LONDON

Rupert Spira

BISHOP'S CASTLE, SHROPSHIRE

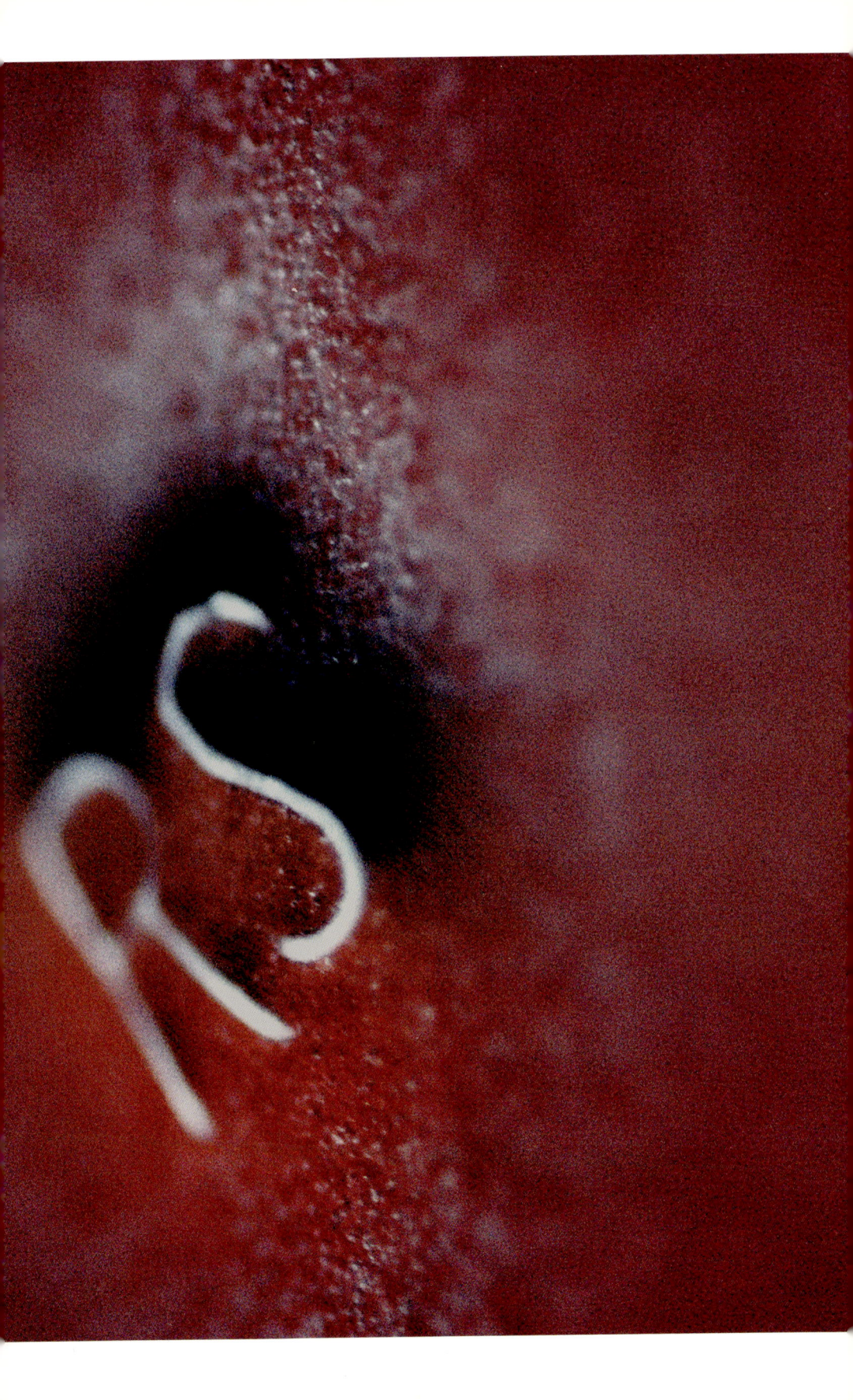

Julian Stair

PECKHAM, LONDON

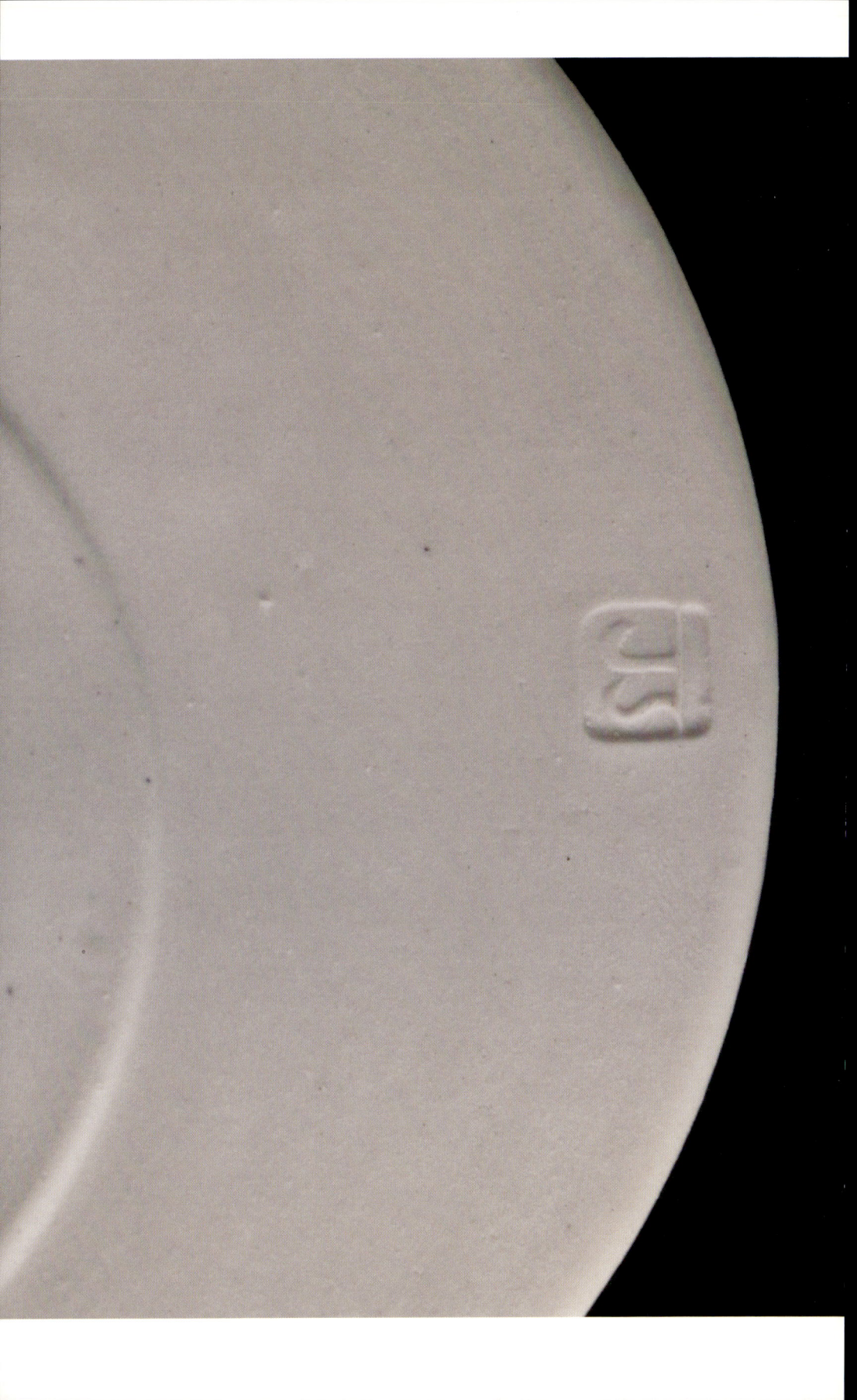

Peter Ting

ROYAL CROWN DERBY, DERBYSHIRE

Takeshi Yasuda

BATH, SOMERSET

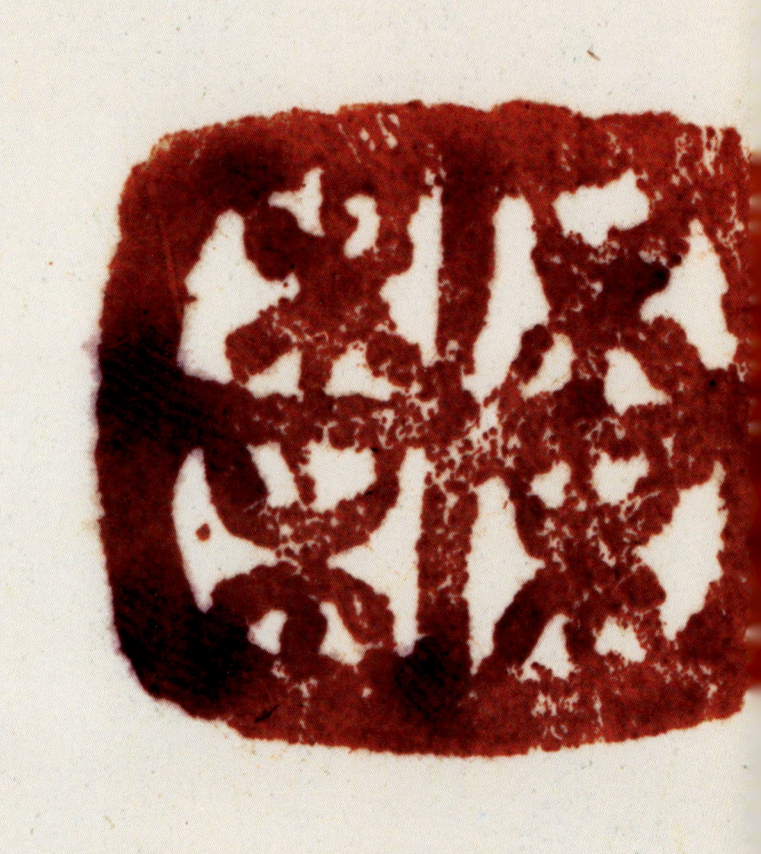

Running Commentary

Alison Britton and Natasha Daintry emailed each other about the progress of their work between January and March 2005. This is an edited version of their correspondence.

AB: I've been slowly working on a pot in the way that I do from time to time. It's like 'cleaning up'; piecing together odd bits of left over clay just to make use of them, waste not want not. I have vaguely in mind a pot I saw in the archaeological museum in Milan just before Christmas, which had three sort of buttresses sticking out of it with figures standing on them. So far I'm doing the ordinary shape underneath, a slightly leaning cylinder and I'm closing it in to the coiled shoulders now.

ND: I like the sound of this pot. As it closes in to the shoulders, do slabs of clay intermingle with coils? How much wall can you build in one go? Unfurling it in your mind's eye must be thrilling because it's bound not to go to plan. I'd like to borrow some of that unknowing. I set off with such a clear idea of what I want to make—five of this and five of that. I wonder if throwing is too prescriptive, or is my throwing too prescripted? I'm in a state of flux at the moment, questioning the fixation I have with usefulness.

Alison Britton | Natasha Daintry

I can't decide if my wish to make useful things links with my days as a language student living in Tokyo when I first fell in love with ceramics. In Japan my home-stay mother was a terrific cook and every evening she would open her white cupboards and choose her dishes and bowls from white industrial china, or rugged country stuff. The straightforward, sensual pleasure of eating delicious things from intriguing, hand- or factory-made ceramics did inspire me.

Or can things be a bit useful just some of the time?

AB: Definitely, and there are so many levels of usefulness involved with human desires and symbols. There's nothing wrong with function—it's the bed-rock of what we are all doing, the underlying point of all artefacts. Opening the cupboard to choose plates for food is still an essential, sophisticated, world-connected and visually exciting pursuit. I've just had glass panels put in my cupboard door so that I can see the stuff better. I love my crockery unreasonably much; I'd rather do all the washing up than risk letting other people mishandle my Masons Ironstone plates with bleeding cobalt painting on.

On the other hand—you could try making something useless and see how it feels?

I've never managed to stick to my intentions when I've tried not to make a container—the pot-ness had to be reinstated. It's a long time though since I threw a pot. I didn't know until later how free it can be—how you can play with the wet sleeve of clay and are not forced to make a circle every time. I envy you the speed of throwing, and the lyricism of touch combined with machine tool, which I think must suit an athletic person like you, full of guts and dash.

The pleasurable state of 'not knowing' is possibly something that grows for artists, and is one of the few perks of getting older.

ND: This is what I am doing next: two opposite things. I want to make some overtly useful bowls, and then think more open-endedly about scale.

The bowls will be quite deep, and you can have soup or stew in them. They will come in sets of two or five. Perhaps they will all be one colour and I would like to think more deeply about how colours can work together as a group. I want to use colour as a material. Donald Judd talked about this. He said there were only three things in art—material, space and colour. I find it strange that people who make white things in clay say that they do this because they are only interested in form. Judd commented on how much writing about his work was in relation to form, scale, minimalism etc, and how his blindingly obvious use of colour was so often ignored! Why should the use of colour preclude an interest in form?

I am doing new colour tests. What interests me just as much as finding fascinating colours is how to use them, how to make them vibrant. Some resonate on their own, like my violent canary yellow glaze. But then there are colours which come alive in relation to what they are put next to. This makes the grouping of things compelling. With my transparent purple-blue glazes, I wanted to convey the feeling of depth, of looking or falling through water.

Thinking about scale, I want to make some huge bowls, huge plates, with as much clay as I can possibly handle. I want to know if that luminous space inside a bowl where the colour hovers, can increase in intensity.

Alison Britton | Natasha Daintry

AB: I'm stuck at the moment with my surfaces—same old glaze, not much conviction to paint marks at present, just a few black crayon lines on recent pieces. It's either powerfully restrained or really boring!

As for building, I normally slab the lower part and coil higher up—just to get more curving movement in the top bit, like shoulders. The buttresses, which I must do next, will be slabbed and attached before I get too closed in or I won't be able to press hard from the inside when I join them on. With soft clay for coiling I don't build very much wall, I'm a bit dilettante in this compared with Gordon Baldwin for instance, who gets out his gas poker and dries it all off and then can build up much faster. I have another piece on the go as well and do a bit of that while I wait. I leave things muffled up in plastic except for the new soft bit overnight, which just has newspaper over it. It suits me to work gradually in this way and have time to change my mind and follow new threads on new days. I'm so much not a designer! More like a rambler.

ND: I think you are an essayist, not a rambler. You make forays around undiscovered or un-signposted parts of cities. Rambling suggests incoherence whereas you have always walked purposefully into unknown parts. What you do is the antithesis of design, which is about control at the point of making. There comes that moment of commitment when you can't change your mind any more. Whereas you go on responding and readjusting until the very end of making.

I'd like to bring some of that freedom into my throwing. Throwing has speed, as you say. This is very appealing to me as I find the physicality of motion intoxicating; swimming lengths, snowboarding, kite-surfing. The languid vigour of swimming, for example, isn't matched by many things. Everything narrows down to breathing in and breathing out, muscles are working, water is being churned and in the middle is an intense concentration. I'd like to achieve this in my throwing, but only rarely manage to.

AB: Going back to surfaces, what do I want to achieve? It's pathetic to have always stuck to the matt clear glaze. Neither dry nor luscious. I'd like more juice, not everywhere but in parts. I'd like to try blotting out parts of the slip painting by re-firing with some things obscured by an opaque glaze with a different character. I think a general kind of mattness, without being too boringly uniform, is probably right for the formal changes. My pots look awful if they turn out shiny. I've been wondering how I could change the system—pouring the inside of a piece and then spraying the outside. I find spraying increasingly less appealing to do. It would be good to paint on glaze with big brushes and have it blend together in the firing. I'd like some time without deadlines to play around with other temperatures—going higher for instance.

The last few pieces have been off-white and black, with some marks like writing—recently one was called 'Scrawl' and one 'Script'. I've just made a handwritten list—thick writing —of titles I still like that I've used in the last few years, like 'trough' and 'side issue'; to have a stencil cut of them all strung together. I'm going to paint dark slip through it onto a sheet of clay. Then I'll paint over it with a lighter slip to make it blurred and less readable. I want to use a couple of sheets in a big cylindrical piece,with ripples deeper at the bottom, so the shape seems to flare out overall.

I've started a new piece—it's waiting to have its extremities attached. It is a flaring-to-the-top square form with half-pipe corners. The top will be covered over, and an opening somewhere on the edge of that square, that slides down over the shoulder. And low feet. There's not much on the surface so far—there were acanthus leaves stencilled on the clay in a pale slip that may have disappeared by the end.

ND: It's funny that I'm harping on about colour while you are heading towards the graphic black and white. I'm interested in the way your scrawl or acanthus leaves begin definite then fade. I have in mind a description of Cy Twombly's drawings which seem simultaneously to press down and at the same time erase themselves. I like the solidity of your buttresses and troughs bearing witness to faint scratchings.

Will you say more about asymmetry and disruption? And round things, is it that circles are too satisfyingly complete? That they lack edginess or interest?

AB: I suppose I love the circles of cups and plates and bowls, but also like to have some ovals and oblongs in the picture, odd shapes like Japanese Oribe stuff. I like circles more when they have distorted a little. The almost perfection is more interesting; I think I avoid absolutes and strivings for exactness through all aspects of life. What William Newland (the first potter I knew) called 'the drover's road not the autobahn'. In other terms is it a poetry/prose distinction? Creased linen rather than starched linen? I still feel more comfortable standing with my weight on one leg so I'm not symmetrical. It feels less stiff (school assembly) and more receptive, wayward, interesting. So the high fired cups with heat distortions are the ones I pick out. Am about to make a cappuccino in an ovalled porcelain cup of Ashley Howard's. But I can love work that is perfectly circular; Maria van Kesteren the Dutch wood turner, Martin Smith, you. But one of the things I really liked about Takeshi's new work was how off-circular they mostly were.

ND: I understand about the drover's road or the autobahn. I've started playing with a single line of colour cutting through or wrapping a whole pot. It travels up, in and under. Visually, it disrupts. I've been thinking about energy channels mapping the body and where and why things get stuck. Sometimes this line is continuous, or it just falls short. I'm also looking at pattern and have a wild desire to cover a bowl in, around and under with it.

I'm getting clearer about usefulness too. You can use my work, but actually in the three years that I've been making it, I've never used a single piece. I've only ever developed glazes safe for food but still my plates are too small, or the large plates too heavy…. I've been trying to squeeze too many concerns into too few pieces. I'd like to crack this nut. I'm hoping that making an overtly useful piece will help me resolve things. This bowl then, needs to be the right size for the job. Already my trials are studies in concentration—of lips, feet, weight and rims.

I picked up some bowls by Karen Downing and Chris Keenan the other day, and they felt like an invitation. Something about the weight and a certain generous unobtrusiveness. They made me want to get home, get cooking and eat. I've made a few of my own bowls now and they do carry a certain lightness and straightforwardness of intention.

So that is that. I've made heavy weather of this stuff since I began ceramics, but there it is.

AB: The strong feelings I have about my own cups connect with your passion about function/beauty/food/throwing. It is enviable, in a way. I just seem to find myself making other things, too big to be useful, occasionally holding flowers or more likely branches.

148 The body and the building as intermingled subjects are still the 'containing' point of it for me, another motivation as strong as the function one.

Perhaps my drift to big and bigger needs disrupting. I've been thinking about horizontals, and legs, and otherwise pipes still seem to be interesting me as relief, enlivening bits.

The black and white surface is not where I want to get stuck, I'm on the way back to colour now I think. I've been looking at yellows a lot with desire.

ND: I want to explore colour using my new bowls. Can a row of them be passionate and quick? Can they have verve and dash? Is the rim fine enough to achieve a floating white halo, but robust enough for stacking?

With my useful bowl in existence, perhaps I can be more free. I have also moved beyond a deluge of technical dramas. I've worked out how to apply glaze thickly, how to achieve that pivot where a piece spirals upwards to a translucent rim and glaze rolls like liquid around bases. I have decided to go back to basics. I've started throwing with my eyes closed. I'm mesmerised by that feeling of stillness within motion.

Barrett Marsden

Barrett Marsden Gallery was set up in Clerkenwell, London, in 1998, by three partners: Tatjana Marsden, Juliana Barrett and Nelson Woo. Marsden's interest in the applied arts started in the 1970s as a silver-smithing student at the Royal College of Art, where she met some of the practitioners the gallery now exhibits. After working for the cutler David Mellor, she definitively established the Craft Council shop at the Victoria & Albert Museum in 1981. She and Juliana Barrett subsequently met when they worked together at Contemporary Applied Arts, of which Marsden was the director until 1990. Here two of the gallery partners discuss the role of their gallery within the context of today's art market.

TM: What I feel is that we're not just a gallery, or a shop, or a business. Our aspirations are higher. When we first met, and Nelson was an inspired collector on the circuit, there were many more interesting private enterprises than there are now. I think our opening finally happened in 1998 because we all felt the moment was right. And as for categories, the divide between fine and applied art or craft, I think that we hate divisions but in many ways we're also glad of them. It's like having a garden fence—you don't necessarily like it, but it helps define things! Interestingly we're in between and it's true that some of our artists could be seen as fine artists.

JB: We both initially said we'd never have a gallery of our own,

Juliana Barrett | Tatjana Marsden

it would be too big an undertaking and too risky financially, but then we thought we'd never know without trying. We already knew the artists we wanted to show—they were there in our heads. Of course new people approach us but we often have to turn them down if their work doesn't fit the overall philosophy.

TM: Our philosophy is to show only what we like and we're very rigid in that. The way we select is part of us—it's our flesh and bones. The gallery has worked because of our priorities and ideology. The commercial side isn't the main aim; if it were, we wouldn't be showing what we do. No other applied arts gallery exhibits quite what we do, we desperately want the artists to remain uncompromising.

We don't only show ceramics, we have work in glass, metal, wood, textile. If someone proposes something unique, we'll always consider it, as it could really add something creative to the mix, like the installation Caroline Broadhead made for a dance performance. We gave Tord Boontje a solo show as a one-off, and last year showed a collaboration between Hans Stofer and the Dutch designer Jair Straschnow. What we show embodies a particular vision, a way of thinking.

JB: We now represent seventeen artists mostly based in the UK—including Gordon Baldwin, Alison Britton, Ken Eastman and Martin Smith who are shown in 'to hold'. All our artists are interestingly different. If I didn't work here, I'd think it was worth crossing London to see the range of shows.

TM: Our artists may all work in different directions but I think together they give a comprehensive insight into what is going on in applied arts. It's about the here and now. Maybe we'll leave a mark because of this and because we genuinely show our aesthetic. The result is that people either love us or hate us! We are trying to do something unique.

JB: And that makes us quite vulnerable. But an important part of our aim is to encourage people to look at things differently. There is a new generation that is open to it too and is becoming part of our audience. People who come to the gallery are not all experts or particularly knowledgeable. Many students are brought by tutors from all over the country—so in this way we're playing an educational role. We've specialised in one person shows which gives the chance to really understand someone's work, which the Crafts Council tends not to. And if we make it possible for just one person to contemplate the work in depth, then it's worth it.

TM: It's an obsessive role and means we are permanently questioning things. We are driven by this belief. It's what I dream about and think about most of the time—then I get to work and walk around the gallery and see all the cracks in the wall that no one else can see!

JB: I suppose you could say that we suffer from perfectionism. We never congratulate ourselves. We know that this is the only way we can do it and we're always trying to do it better. Although there may be a moment when we've finished installing a show, when the lighting is done and we say "that looks good". But the point of it isn't about our input, it's about the artist's work.

Juliana Barrett | Tatjana Marsden

TM: With regard to giving opportunities to artists, you have to make a choice in the end. Most successful galleries show only a few artists to give a real sense of direction. That really helps the public and the collectors. Our buyers come from all over the world—the only common denominator is an interest in applied arts, and we try to guide them within that. We have a lot of visitors from America, Germany, Holland and Denmark—and some from France. But those European countries stand out because the Germans and Scandinavians and Dutch in particular have a strong applied arts scene of their own, and there has been good interaction with British exhibitors, so they know what they're looking at.

JB: Museums also buy from us—though not as much as we'd like! Recent purchases have been from the V&A, the Crafts Council, Liverpool, Aberdeen, Stoke-on-Trent, and the Musèe des Arts Dècoratifs in Paris and the National Gallery of Australia in Canberra. Our artists are well known in this field. But museums only buy sporadically, budgets are very constrained, we mail them frequently but can't always expect a response.

TM: We're not exactly well-travelled, in fact we hardly move! We'd like to do more exchanges with galleries abroad. Our stable is not all British, although for practical reasons they are the majority. We work with three Dutch artists and represent one of them, and we have had projects with galleries in the States, Holland, and Germany.

JB: We also show at the American art-fair SOFA (Sculptural Objects Functional Art) in Chicago every autumn. That gives us different exposure. America has a very enthusiastic market but it has dropped since 9|11. Americans have enormous respect for British applied art, they look for its subtlety. There is a strong group of European and British collectors too; and this year we also showed at Collect at the V&A.

TM: There's also the tourism element. Americans love coming to London and art-shopping at the same time. I think because of the nature of our business, mail order hardly ever works; we are not selling for investment. Most of the objects we sell are picked with considerable intensity and care by our clients. Looking, touching, and comparing is part of the process of acquisition.

JB: What some of the work needs is a different approach from potential buyers, not just technical questions about how a piece is made, whether it's thrown or how it's glazed. In most cases those details are irrelevant, the work is about the content. When we show a jug we're not necessarily interested in its function. It would be wonderful to get more corporate clients, we need to encourage their art advisors to think seriously about this kind of work. We've put together so many commercially viable portfolios for them, but in the end the advisors often tend to buy painting students' work for their clients, something you can hang on the wall.

TM: It does help us to analyse where the applied arts are placed, what the public misconceptions are and what we are up against. But we wouldn't be here if we didn't think things could change and that we could contribute something—even if we're seen at the moment as being "too classy"! I don't want to be seen as a fine art gallery because I don't think it's appropriate or has any greater kudos.

JB: Nothing's perfect. In some ways we are limited, there just aren't enough hours in the day and we would also love to have a larger space. We're not complacent, we're always thinking of how we could do a better job for the artists.

TM: At least we can say that we constantly strive for more and we're artist-driven; we're here for them, they are our friends. We don't employ anyone else in the gallery, and that makes it quite hard, but it means that whoever comes in can have an intelligent conversation about the work based on real understanding and background, on fact rather than fiction and hype!

The Collector

Collecting ceramics: why? who? how? where? In considering these ${155}$ questions, Harriet K. outlines the process and philosophy behind building up her collection. Ceramics for her can have as much aesthetic presence as works in any other medium. It is a universal and ancient craft. Her collection also includes paintings and furniture, but ceramics are her strongest preoccupation. She has been acquiring pots for at least twenty-five years.

As a teenager I was keen to do art at school but, not being able to draw, I ended up doing pottery, which I found I loved. That early experience and contact with clay left me with a sharpened sensitivity about pots. I'm very aware of the objects themselves and of the motivation behind them. My creativity now goes into choosing and displaying pots.

I started collecting as soon as I left school, when I discovered the British Crafts Centre in Covent Garden. The very first pot I bought was by John Ward. It is small and fine and fits into the hand, it seduced me with its sombre colours and the depth of surface. I still love these black surfaces, the flatness and density, the variety within them, and the glimpse of metals showing through. It was not expensive; I was only a student at the time and couldn't spend much. What is remarkable is that twenty years later I still love this piece, there is something both perfect and imperfect about it; it is coiled not thrown. I have some red clay pieces of Elspeth Owen's that have a similar warmth and tactility. The thrown pieces I respond to are often quite fluid, the potter letting the form err without losing control. My large Edmund de Waal pieces have this quality, and I have an unusual grey lidded jar of his as well.

Other early purchases came from Atmosphere Gallery which was near where I lived in the seventies. I bought Nick Homoky pieces there, crisp white bowls with witty drawings, and the splashily coloured stoneware jug by Janice Tchalenko. I was often visiting Oxford then too and first saw Lucie Rie pieces at the Oxford Gallery. When Tatjana Marsden was working in the Crafts Council shop at the V&A in the eighties, that was a very good place to buy. She had a way of never imposing herself but you felt you could ask all kinds of questions.

Nearly everything in my collection is a container, whether I use it or not. I think of my pieces as one collection, but some things are in the kitchen and are in constant use like my Batterham coffee pots, and other pieces are one-off more sculptural things. The domestic realm includes cups, beakers, jugs, jars and mugs by Edmund de Waal, Julian Stair, Wally Keeler, Chris Keenan, Sarah Walton, Carina Ciscato, Richard Batterham, and plates by Rupert Spira. If the piece is some kind of drinking vessel the way in which it functions is really important to me. The lip should be thin, and the size and shape can help keep the coffee hot. The sensations of use alter visual perception—or is it vice versa? For example I have a set of terracotta espresso cups by Julian Stair, raw and smooth on the outside and with a taupe glazed interior. They sit in quite deep saucers which could be seen as being out of proportion. But it's that offbeat relationship that I love. It means you never take them for granted, they always have an effect on you.

Not everything I drink out of is handmade, I have a wonderful set of fine shallow porcelain cups and saucers from Arzberg which are exactly right for drinking tea. On top of the crockery cupboard are some occasionally used things like jars by Jim Malone, the sharp spouted large blue-grey jug by Wally Keeler, and a spiral storage jar of his; (and I regret not buying a salt glazed teapot when I could have).

The other pots spread into almost every room of the house. John Ward, Lucy Rie, Joanna Constantinidis, and Gordon Baldwin all feature very strongly, and I have two wonderful groups of pieces by Gwyn Hanssen Pigott. The first was shown in her *Still Lives* exhibition at Galerie Besson in 1992, at the start of her new way of working. Then in 2000 I acquired this much larger group from Besson that is more like a procession than a cluster. It is called *Still Life with Blue Beaker* and is made up of twelve bottles, bowls and beakers (one blue) with one perfect cup, all in slightly different tones of pale glazed porcelain. I lent it to her exhibition at Tate St Ives in 2004.

Sometimes my decision to buy is very spontaneous, it's a gut-feeling. In the early eighties in the British Crafts Centre I saw this unusually large, square, slab-built porcelain pot with a fine blue scratched drawing all over it, by Masamichi Yoshikawa, who was unknown here at the time. It's still a very important piece for me, and in 1998 I curated a small exhibition of his work at the DAIWA Foundation in Regents Park.

In a more deliberate way I knew I wanted to buy a piece of Nick Rena's some years ago and went to the Oxford Gallery especially, and chose this dark red bowl. I have wondered

Harriet K.

about the colour since, I now also have a deep blue jug form and a more recent horizontal white piece from his last exhibition. Colour is very significant for me, I would never buy anything yellow.

Of course there are things I've missed. I wish I owned a Hans Coper, a Lawson Oyekan, a Ken Eastman when he made smaller things. I'd like a Prue Venables piece, an Alison Britton, and a recent Takeshi Yasuda.

A lot of younger potters seem to me less exciting than the older generation. An exception is this new piece by James Evans with its shiny white crackled glaze and ambiguous form.

It is rare for me to get to know the makers, I don't feel that I will ask the right questions, but I like to understand what lies behind the creative process. I met Edmund de Waal first at Chelsea Craft Fair and bought his beautiful tapered beakers, before he began to make the large cylinder forms that I have since collected, or started his work with installation. It has been a rewarding connection, he has been so thoughtful and encouraging, about the DAIWA Foundation exhibition for instance. I would like to do this sort of thing again, especially if I could co-organise it with someone else. I'd like to show the young Brazilian potter Carina Ciscato.

In the end I never think about the monetary value of a piece, only its visual value. But price comes into the choosing process inevitably and I don't have a lot to spend. The prices for established names have risen of course, a Gordon Baldwin now costs £3000–4000, so I arrange to pay in instalments.

I'm not keen on private views as it is harder to see the

work, the crowd adds to the pressure. I like to see something, go away and think, come back and maybe change my mind. I try to visualise its place in my collection.

Some galleries are much more enjoyable to buy from than others. I like to be quietly left alone to see the pieces for myself. You can have a good conversation with some gallerists, but this is rare. The beauty of the place is also part of the whole experience.

Nowadays I save up to buy the pieces I really want. After his 1999 solo show, seen in the wonderful uncluttered Barrett Marsden space, I realised that Gordon Baldwin is vital to my collection, and I must follow him seriously however difficult that is. So I plan more and fewer major purchases, and try not to be tempted by the easily affordable things. Baldwin's pieces never disappoint. I would love to have a drawing of his as well; he showed both in his last exhibition.

One should be able to pick up and feel pottery, not just admire it from a distance. There may be moments when you don't 'see' things, but that is because of the way we live, with little time to sit and look. I really enjoy having the red bowl of Nick Rena's behind me in my office, I can almost feel it there. It's important to find a way for things to work together, for example I have put this Baldwin black and white piece near a drawing because they give something to each other. When I converted the house I thought about possibilities for display. It takes time to find the right place for each piece, I try things out in different rooms. We use the high ledges on the steel beams in the extension into the garden where the daylight is very strong. I have just moved the large Hanssen Pigott group from a mantelpiece upstairs into this room and it has come to

Harriet K.

life, flooded with light and at a lower level where you can see into the beakers. If you have the clarity to contemplate then that's fine—that is the bottom line.

A collection is an expression of a person, it grows with you. If I had to choose one piece to rescue, it would have to be the Lucie Rie bowl that I have had for so long. It flares up from a narrow base, is light, and glazed a greenish white with a blurred metallic line around its sharp elegant rim.'

To Hold

A reflection on the vessel and the title of the exhibition by Alun Graves, Curator of Ceramics and Glass at the Victoria & Albert Museum, London.

To hold. An apparently simple act of containment, but one redolent of rich and layered meaning, suggestive of relationship, of protector and protected, and thus of care, of intimacy, of secret interior spaces, of privacy, of possession.

The act of containment is fundamental to ceramics. It is the attribute that, perhaps above all others, defines what a ceramic work is about. It is almost invariably the first question one asks of a ceramic object. Does it contain? Is it a vessel? The role of pottery as containers is as old as pottery itself. From Neolithic storage pots to Etruscan cinerary vases to the teawares of the 18th century, ceramics embody roles that are fundamental to life, or indeed stand as containers of life (or death) itself. And it is clear too, that these roles range from the practical and utilitarian to the ceremonial and precious. What is perhaps more surprising is that in today's world of ceramic art, where makers might be thought to have unlimited freedom of expression, the theme of the vessel remains such an urgent one. One only has to contemplate the title of a work such as Gordon Baldwin's *Vessel for Dark Air*, to sense the potential metaphorical significance of the act of containment.

For a number of makers who reached maturity in the 1970s, artists like Alison Britton and others who shared her concerns,

Alun Graves

the vessel was—and remains—of primary significance. It provided the vehicle for a modernist investigation of the medium itself, works that both were, and were about, ceramics. As a form, the vessel provided a means of retaining some semblance of function, while at the same time, through physical manipulation or distortion, querying it. Boldly self-referential, these were objects that, as Britton suggested, gave more than was demanded of them. Vessels became containers of meaning, and of ideas. Yet beyond this more intellectual approach, there remained something quite basic about the human relationship with ceramic vessels. This, Britton recognised to be the root of their power. Vessels are basic, archetypal, and timeless. They form part of the fundamental material culture of civilisation. Their relationship to people is inherent and specific.

Our expectation of containment within ceramics is perhaps reinforced by the word 'pot' itself: that most fundamental of descriptors that can stand for a range of more specific forms. Indeed the more simplified in form a vessel becomes, the more one wishes to call it by that name. Even the form of the word itself, beautiful in its compactness, suggests containment: a well bounded by sides. And to me it carries an onomatopoeic ring: a hollow, spacious sound, resounding from a rap on the wall of ceramic jar. A pot, to pot, the potter. The shared derivation secures the relationships. A potter by definition makes pots. By extension, a ceramicist can be expected to be the maker of ceramic vessels.

This may sound a touch trite. Yet it is, to some considerable extent, borne out by practice. Despite the ambition of today's generation of makers, despite the shifting and crossing of boundaries, despite the interest in installation-based work and the increasingly sculptural nature of much output, the making of pots remains at the core of much ceramic practice. To some extent, of course, containment in ceramics is a technical inevitability, a logical outcome of their processes of manufacture, of coiling, or throwing on the wheel, or building from slabs. And similarly, their hollowness, or flatness, with openings to any interior spaces, is born of necessity, allowing the clay to dry evenly and the forms to withstand the rigours of firing. Yet it is revealing to note that, by and large, such technical requirements are worn openly, often becoming significant aesthetic or conceptual elements of the work. Even the most supremely sculptural and rarefied of Hans Coper's works, his Cycladic forms, retained their vessel nature, their hollowness and capacity for containment unambiguously stated by an albeit tiny yet conventional mouth at their uppermost point. Similarly, the openings cut through to the interiors of Gordon Baldwin's otherwise enclosed sculptural forms are significant surface events, points of incident that mark the meeting of spaces of fundamentally different character. Even in the case of Felicity Aylieff who, prior to her recent return to the vessel, offered no visible sight of the interior spaces of her forms, nevertheless remained preoccupied with the suggestion of what lay within.

This exhibition, which celebrates the act of containment, reinforces the centrality of vessel forms. The range of work is both stylistically and technically diverse, and the concerns of the different makers are varied, yet the theme of the vessel is common to all. For most, function is likewise an important element, although the expectation of practical use, of active physical participation in our domestic lives, varies considerably. For some, function remains theoretical, and

Alun Graves

containment conceptual. Yet for others, the possibility of physical interaction with the works is of prime importance. Thus the container becomes the contained, and in this shifting of roles, the concept 'to hold' takes on a different aspect.

There is, I believe, something specific and engaging about handling the hand-made object. Through its use, a direct link is formed between maker and consumer. The thoughts and ideas of the potter, laid down by physical manipulation of the material, are read directly through touch. As a method of communication it is extraordinarily direct, almost visceral, and mediated only by the object itself. Especially satisfying are the instances where, despite the transformative nature of firing, something of the plasticity of the raw clay is captured in the finished work. Takeshi Yasuda is particularly successful in this respect, his pots eloquently describing the physical properties of clay. In character, such works are generous and revealing.

The recognition of the importance of touch as a method of experiencing ceramics—the awareness of their haptic potential—has provided an additional rationale for the making of functional pottery. Combined with this comes an increasing appreciation of its ceremonial possibilities. A functional pot is not necessarily an everyday pot. It can be a marker of occasions, of moments of celebration, a symbol of hospitality and of sharing. Or it can help to reinforce the importance of rituals of eating and drinking, encouraging pause for thought. This seems of considerable importance, one of a number of ways in which to counter the widespread trivialisation of food in our society. The capacity of pottery to function in these ways, to give more than their basic requirements demand of them, has consequences for their economics of production. It may be unrealistic for a potter to produce wares at prices that would readily allow everyday use. But if the added value of the artist maker is perceived, the equations may perhaps be differently drawn. Pricing is inevitably contentious, yet it is worth reflecting on why it seems that the possibility that an object could be used should necessarily lessen its value. The implication is that such objects are aesthetically or intellectually inferior, yet if one considers, say, a Walter Keeler teapot, the validity of this argument is hard to accept.

Another change that may be to the benefit of makers of functional wares is the alteration in our attitudes towards tableware in general. There is today little expectation that anyone should hold a complete matching dinner service, and industrial producers seem to have begun to accept that consumers may wish to buy only a few pieces from a range, mixing and matching these with other items, and using them as they see fit. Such changes seem very much to the advantage of independent makers, who may be little able to produce entire services even if they wished to, and whose strength lies in their capability to create individual pieces of beauty and distinction. The depth and quality of functional pottery among contemporary makers, attested to by this exhibition, and also convincingly demonstrated by the recent *Table Manners* show at the Crafts Council, suggests there is much to be optimistic about. The field is wide open.

Whether for action, or reflection, or indeed both, ceramic vessels continue to hold a fundamental place in our lives. They satisfy some of our most basic needs, and fulfil roles charged with significance. They are both ubiquitous and extraordinary. To make ceramic vessels is to participate in a tradition of almost unimaginable length and complexity. Yet their capacity to hold, and to be held, remains basic, timeless, and enduring.

Alun Graves

166

TO HOLD

Contacts

Felicity Aylieff
Garden Flat, 14 Grosvenor Place
Bath BA1 6AX
Telephone: 07714 212124
felicity.aylieff@rca.ac.uk |
aylieff@btinternet.com

Gordon Baldwin
Barrett Marsden Gallery
17–18 Great Sutton Street
London EC1V 0DN
Telephone: 020 7336 6396
info@bmgallery.co.uk
www.bmgallery.co.uk

Jan Baldwin
11 Gibraltar Walk
London E2 7LH
Telephone: 020 7729 2664
studio@janbaldwin.co.uk
www.janbaldwin.co.uk

Barrett Marsden Gallery
17–18 Great Sutton Street
London EC1V 0DN
Telephone: 020 7336 6396
info@bmgallery.co.uk
www.bmgallery.co.uk

Alison Britton
Barrett Marsden Gallery
17–18 Great Sutton Street
London EC1V 0DN
Telephone: 020 7336 6396
info@bmgallery.co.uk
www.bmgallery.co.uk

Natasha Daintry
401½ Workshops
401½ Wandsworth Road
London SW8 2JP
Telephone: 020 7582 2531
ndaintry@dsl.pipex.com

Fiona Dunlop
fdunlop@clara.co.uk

Ken Eastman
Barrett Marsden Gallery
17–18 Great Sutton Street
London EC1V 0DN
Telephone: 020 7336 6396
info@bmgallery.co.uk
www.bmgallery.co.uk |
www.keneastman.co.uk

Morgen Hall
Chapter Arts Centre, Market Road
Cardiff CF5 1QE
Telephone: 029 311050 ext.219
morgen@morgenhall.co.uk
www.morgenhall.co.uk

He Jian
c/o 60 Brantwood Road
London SE24 0DJ

Walter Keeler
Moorcroft Cottage, Penallt
Monmouthshire NP25 4AH
Telephone: 01600 713946

Bodil Manz
Kalundborgvej 53
4534 Hørve, Denmark
bodilmanz@mail.dk

Hylton Nel
Michael Stevenson Gallery
Hill House, De Smidt Street
Green Point, Cape Town
South Africa
www.michaelstevenson.com

Margaret O'Rorke
Corpus Christi Farm House
Sandford Road, Littlemore
Oxford OX4 4PX
Telephone: 01865 771653
margaret.ororke@btinternet.com

Royal Crown Derby Porcelain
Company Limited
194 Osmaston Road, Derby DE23 8JZ
Telephone: 01332 712800
enquiries@royalcrownderby.co.uk
www.royalcrownderby.co.uk

Martin Smith
Barrett Marsden Gallery
17–18 Great Sutton Street
London EC1V 0DN
Telephone: 020 7336 6396
info@bmgallery.co.uk
www.bmgallery.co.uk

Rupert Spira
Church Farm, More, Bishop's Castle,
Shropshire SY9 5HH

Julian Stair
127 Court Lane, London SE21 7EE
Telephone: 020 8693 4877
studio@julianstair.com
www.julianstair.com

Peter Ting
60 Brantwood Road
London SE24 0DJ
Telephone: 020 7274 8900
peter.ting@btinternet.com

Takeshi Yasuda
Garden Flat, 14 Grosvenor Place
Bath BA1 6AX
Telephone: 07714 212124
t.yasuda@btinternet.com

Acknowledgements

1. Cork 2005 for initiating this project.
2. OPW and Farmleigh Gallery for giving the exhibition a home.
3. Helen, Nicky, Peter, Tamsyn, Viv and Wayne from Jan Baldwin's studio, your help was invaluable, thank you.
4. Alison Britton, Natasha Daintry, Fiona Dunlop, Barrett Marsden Gallery, Harriet K., and Alun Graves, for your contribution towards the essays.
5. Royal Crown Derby for their sponsorship.
6. Michael Stevenson's long distance coordination between London and Calitzdorp, South Africa.
7. Colin Sackett's sensitive and elegant book design.
8. Vincent O'Shea and Brian Kennedy for their calming and uplifting influences.
9. Last but no means least, thank you to all the makers, who generously allowed myself and Jan to capture a part of their lives.

Peter Ting
London, March 2006

The Office of Public Works
Oifig na nOibreacha Poiblí

FARMLEIGH GALLERY